Written and Illustrated by Caroline Arnold

A Day and Night in the FOREST

PICTURE WINDOW BOOKS
a capstone imprint

Cheerup, cheerup! chirp the robins.

It is a cool spring morning in a North American forest. New leaves cover the trees. Robins are building a nest on a high branch.

A deer nibbles some leaves. Her fawn lies quietly while she eats. The mother deer hears a noise. She snorts and dashes away.

A fawn's white spots help it hide in the dappled shade of the forest.

A squirrel scampers down a tree and digs in the forest floor. It finds an acorn that it buried last fall. The squirrel tucks the acorn into its cheek and runs back up the tree.

Squirrels often bury nuts and seeds to eat later. If the squirrels don't dig them up, the seeds may grow into new trees.

A mother woodchuck munches dandelion leaves. Suddenly she spots a hawk. *Whee-oh! Whee-oh!* she whistles. Her babies dart to safety in their underground den.

At a forest pond, a heron stands quietly and hunts for fish and frogs. It snatches its prey with its long bill. Nearby a box turtle searches for worms and snails. The turtle finds a snail and grabs it with its mouth.

A pair of ducks paddles across the cool water. They tip their heads below the surface and find plants and insects to eat.

Mallards are a kind of duck. Males have green heads. Females are mostly brown.

A garter snake warms itself in a patch of sunlight. Then it slithers along the forest floor. It hides under a log. When a toad hops by, the snake catches it and swallows it whole.

Nearby a mother rabbit and her babies rest under a bush. In the late afternoon, the rabbits will leave their nest. They will hop to the forest edge and eat clover and grass.

A cottontail rabbit has a small white tail that looks like a ball of cotton.

As daylight fades two black bear cubs follow their mother through the forest. The mother bear finds a clump of oak seedlings and nips off the new leaves. When she is done eating, she feeds her cubs milk.

A raccoon peers out of its tree hole. It waits for the bears to leave. Then it climbs down to look for something to eat. It catches a crayfish in a forest stream.

A raccoon's front paws are like little hands. They are good for grasping and holding objects.

The forest grows dark. An owl hears a squeak on the forest floor. A mouse is looking for seeds. The owl swoops down on silent wings and catches its prey.

An opossum wakes up and comes out of its den.
It is hungry too. It digs into a rotten log and
finds juicy grubs and beetles to eat.

Opossums will eat almost anything, including plants,
insects, eggs, worms, garbage, and dead animals.

Near a forest pond, a beaver gnaws on a willow tree. *Crash!* The tree falls down. The beaver snips off a tender branch and eats the twigs. Then the beaver bites off another branch and swims with it to its lodge.

A beaver shelter is called a lodge. It keeps the beavers safe and dry. The entrance to the lodge is underwater.

A moth flutters in the moonlight. Bats flap and glide as they chase insects. Spring peeper frogs call to one another. *Peep, peep! Peep, peep!*

15

A fox prowls in the dark forest shadows. It hears a rustle in the leaves. Is it a mouse? The fox pounces, but the mouse leaps away just in time.

Foxes are hunters, but they also eat fruit and a few plants.

A porcupine climbs a tree, grabbing branches with its feet. It finds twigs and leaves to eat. Sharp quills protect the porcupine from most predators.

The sky grows light as morning comes. Nighttime animals are ready to rest. The fox trots back to its den, bats fly to their roosts, and opossums go into their holes. Daytime animals wake up. Robins chirp, squirrels scamper down trees, and deer feed on fresh leaves at the forest edge.

Every day and every night, animals find food, water, and safe places to rest in the forest. It provides them with everything they need.

What Is a Forest?

A forest is a large area of trees and plants. There are four major types of forests in the world: boreal, coniferous, deciduous, and rain forest. This book is about the deciduous forests of North America.

A deciduous forest has trees that lose their leaves in autumn and grow new leaves in spring. Oaks, maples, hickories, and elms are deciduous trees. Shrubs, leafy plants, and mosses also grow in a deciduous forest.

Plants and animals that live in deciduous forests are adapted to the changing seasons. During cold winter months, some animals hibernate or grow thick fur. Other animals migrate to warmer places.

Throughout the day and night, animals are busy in the forest. Diurnal animals are active during the day. Nocturnal animals are active at night. Which animals in this book are diurnal? Which are nocturnal? Where do they live in the forest?

Where Can You Find Deciduous Forests?

Deciduous forests are found in North America, Europe, Asia, South America, Australia, and New Zealand. They grow in Earth's temperate zones, the areas between the very cold polar zones and the very hot tropical zones.

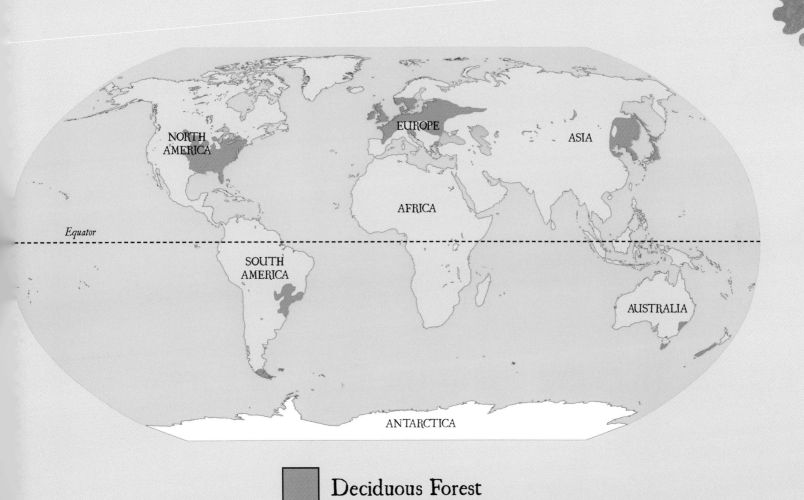

Deciduous Forest

Fun Facts

- Beavers, squirrels, and other rodents have sharp front teeth that never stop growing. Rodents must regularly bite and chew to wear down their teeth.

- Woodchucks are a kind of large rodent. They are also called groundhogs or whistle pigs.

- A duck's feathers are coated with a special oil that makes them waterproof.

- A female cottontail rabbit may have up to seven litters, or groups of babies, each year. There are two to seven baby rabbits in each litter.

- The word "raccoon" comes from an American Indian word meaning "animal that scratches with its hands."

- Opossums use their long tails to hold on while climbing. They can hang from their tails, but only for a short time.

- Spring peeper frogs get their name from the sounds they make in spring. The male frogs "peep" to let females know they are ready to mate.

- A porcupine's body is covered with about 30,000 quills. When a baby porcupine is born, its quills are soft. They harden in about an hour.

Critical Thinking Using the Common Core

1. Describe how the passing of time is shown throughout this book. (Integration of Knowledge and Ideas)

2. Name three diurnal predators in a deciduous forest and their prey. Then name three nocturnal predators and their prey. (Key Ideas and Details)

Glossary

adapt—to change to fit into a new or different environment

boreal—(BOR-ee-uhl) relating to the world's northernmost growing area; birch and poplar are common boreal trees

coniferous—(koh-NIF-er-us) having cones and green, needle-shaped leaves year-round; pines and firs are examples of coniferous trees

crayfish—a freshwater animal that looks like a small lobster

dappled—spotty

deciduous—(dih-SIJ-oo-us) having leaves that fall off every year; maples and oaks are examples of deciduous trees

diurnal—active during the day

grub—a young insect in larval form; it looks like a short, fat worm

habitat—the natural home or environment of an animal, plant, or other living thing

hibernate—to spend winter in a deep sleep; animals hibernate to survive low temperatures and lack of food

mate—to join together to produce young

migrate—to move from one place to another on a seasonal basis

nocturnal—active at night

predator—an animal that hunts other animals for food

prey—an animal hunted by another animal for food

rodent—an animal with long front teeth used for gnawing; rats, mice, and squirrels are examples of rodents

roost—a place where birds sit and bats can hang and rest

Read More

Andrews, Alexa. *In the Forest*. Penguin Young Readers. New York: Penguin Young Readers, an imprint of Penguin Group (USA) Inc.: 2013.

Llewellyn, Claire. *Forests*. Habitat Survival. Chicago: Raintree, 2013.

Sill, Cathryn. *About Habitats: Forests*. About Habitats. Atlanta: Peachtree Publishers, 2014.

Index

Internet Sites

FactHound offers a safe, fun way to find Internet sites related to this book. All of the sites on FactHound have been researched by our staff.

Here's all you do:

Visit *www.facthound.com*

Type in this code: 9781479560752

Super-cool stuff! Check out projects, games and lots more at www.capstonekids.com

Special thanks to our adviser for his expertise:

Terry Flaherty, PhD, Professor of English
Minnesota State University, Mankato

Editor: Jill Kalz
Designer: Lori Bye
Art Director: Nathan Gassman
Production Specialist: Kathy McColley
The illustrations in this book were created with cut paper.
Design Elements: Shutterstock/Alfondo de Tomas (map),
    Alvaro Cabrera Jimenez

Picture Window Books are published by Capstone,
1710 Roe Crest Drive, North Mankato, Minnesota 56003
www.capstonepub.com

Library of Congress Cataloging-in-Publication Data
Arnold, Caroline, author, illustrator.
  A day and night in the forest / written and illustrated by Caroline Arnold.
     pages cm.—(Nonfiction picture books. Caroline Arnold's habitats)
  Summary: "Highlights the activities of animals in a North American deciduous forest during one average 24-hour period"—Provided by publisher.
  Audience: K to grade 3.
  Includes bibliographical references and index.
  ISBN 978-1-4795-6075-2 (library binding)
  ISBN 978-1-4795-6087-5 (paperback)
  ISBN 978-1-4795-6147-6 (eBook PDF)
1. Forest animals—Behavior—North America—Juvenile literature.
2. Forest animals—North America—Juvenile literature. I. Title.
  QL112.A76 2015
  591.73097—dc23   2014025334

Look for all the books in the series:

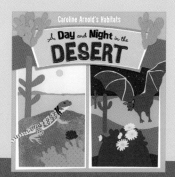

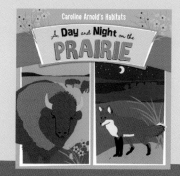

Printed in the United States of America in North Mankato, Minnesota   092014   008482CGS15